GOAL II
LIVING THE DREAM

LEVEL 1

SCHOLASTIC

Adapted by: Penny Hancock

Publisher: Jacquie Bloese

Editor: Jane Rollason

Designer: Mo Choy

Picture research: Emma Bree

Photo credits:

Page 5: D. Hall/Alamy; M. Cristofori/Corbis.
Pages 34 & 35: K. Dannemiller/Corbis; B. Birmelin/Milkshake Films; V. Valitutti, D. Hogan, P. P. Marcou/AFP/Getty Images; H. Gerald/Empics.
Pages 36 & 37: J. Giles, J. Giddens/Empics; D Faget/AFP, P. Armestre, B. Radfors, D. Doyle, A. Want/Getty Images; R. Morris, Euro Press/Alamy; J. Hicks/Corbis.

Mary Glasgow Magazines (Scholastic Ltd.)

Euston House

24 Eversholt Street

London

NW1 1DB

Printed in Singapore. Reprinted in 2008.

CONTENTS

Santiago Muñez is Mexican. His family went to Los Angeles when he was twelve. His grandmother and brother still live there. Santiago is a footballer. He plays for Newcastle United FC in the north-east of England. His friends call him Santi.

Roz Harmison works in a hospital in Newcastle. She is Santi's girlfriend. They have a lovely house in Newcastle. She loves Santi but she doesn't love his money.

Gavin Harris is Santi's friend. Gavin played for Newcastle United in *Goal I*, but now he plays for Real Madrid. He loves parties and clubs. He's not very clever with money.

Jordana García works for Spanish TV. She is very beautiful.

Rudi Van der Merwe is the Real Madrid coach.

Rosa Maria lives in a poor part of Madrid. She lives with her husband and her son and they have a small bar. They all love Real Madrid.

Enrique is Rosa Maria's son. He wants to be a footballer.

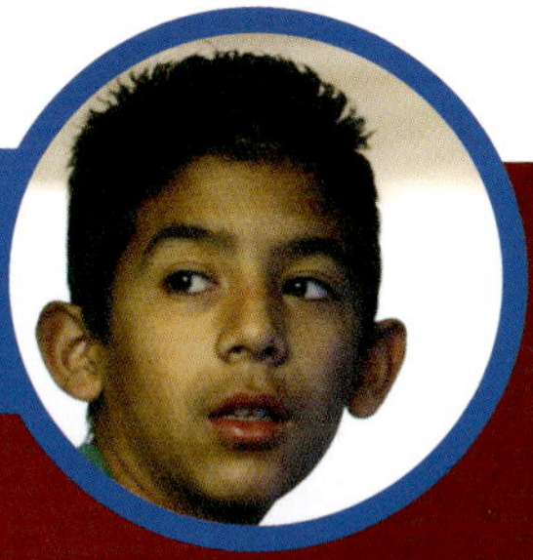

PLACES

Newcastle is a big city in the north-east of England. It is cold in the winter but it has a good night life in the summer. People from Newcastle have a special name – 'Geordies'. Newcastle United FC play at St James' Park in the middle of the city.

Madrid is a big city in the centre of Spain. It's very hot here in the summer. People from Madrid are Madrileños. Real Madrid play at the Bernabéu in Madrid.

The Buddha bar is in Madrid. The Real footballers often come here after a football game. Madrid has a great night life.

GOAL II
LIVING THE DREAM

CHAPTER 1
Newcastle

'Goal!' Everyone shouted when Santiago scored.

The Newcastle United fans loved Santiago Muñez. He scored goals all the time.

And Santiago loved Newcastle. It rained a lot, and it was often cold. But he had a beautiful home, a fantastic BMW car and cool clothes. He also had a great girlfriend. Her name was Roz.

Santiago came from a poor part of Mexico. His mother left home when he was a boy. Then his father took the family to the USA. Santi lived with his father, grandmother and little brother in Los Angeles. They were very poor. Santi worked hard for his father in the day. In the evenings, he played football. He loved football. One evening a man from England watched Santi. His name was Glen Foy and he was on holiday in Los Angeles. When Glen was younger, he was a famous footballer. He played for Newcastle United. He thought that Santiago was fantastic!

'Come and play football in England,' said Glen. 'Come and talk to Newcastle United.'

Newcastle United! A top Premiership* team!

* England's top 20 teams play in the Premiership.

So Santiago went to Newcastle. He played well. He scored goals. The team liked him. Life was good for Santiago and Santiago was good for Newcastle United.

***

Some men in Madrid watched Santiago on TV. They saw the goal.

'He's a great footballer,' one man said. 'How many goals did he score this year?'

'Twenty-eight,' said the other man. 'Let's talk to him.'

***

That evening Santiago and Roz went to an Indian restaurant with some friends. Then Glen Foy came into the restaurant.

'Glen,' said Santi. 'Come and sit with us.'

'Santi, can I talk to you for a minute?' Glen asked.

'Oh, OK,' said Santiago. He looked at Roz and their friends. 'Excuse me,' he said.

Santi followed Glen to the back of the restaurant.

'Listen!' said Glen. 'I had a phone call. Are you ready for this? It was Real Madrid. They like you. They want to meet you.'

'I don't believe it!' thought Santiago. 'Real Madrid! I'm dreaming!'

***

Later that evening, Santi told Roz about Real.

'But you're happy here in Newcastle,' she said.

'I know. I've got this beautiful house and a great job. I've got you. I've got everything.'

'And you're Newcastle United's best player.'

'Maybe,' he said. 'But this is Real Madrid! The best team in the world. Who do I choose? Newcastle or Real Madrid?'

CHAPTER 2
Tokyo

'Real Madrid are in Tokyo. We're flying there tomorrow,' said Glen to Santiago.

'Tomorrow?' said Santiago.

'People work fast in football,' said Glen.

***

Santiago and Glen arrived at the Park Hyatt Hotel in Tokyo. Santi's hotel room was very cool and he wanted to have a bath. But then Glen called.

'They want to talk to us now,' he said.

Santi went to meet the men from Real. He was nervous. There was the coach, Rudi Van der Merwe, and the two top men, Florentino Pérez and Señor Burruchaga.

'We watch you play a lot,' said Burruchaga. 'You're good.'

'I'm lucky,' said Santi. 'I play for a great team.'

Señor Pérez liked Santi's answer.

'We want you at Real Madrid. Come and play for us!'

'Wow!' thought Santiago. 'This is very exciting.' But he also felt frightened.

'Yes,' he thought, 'I want to play for Real. Every footballer in the world wants to play for Real. But I want to play football. I don't want to sit on the bench. And what about Roz?'

'You must decide quickly,' said Burruchaga. 'Give us your answer by midnight tomorrow.'

***

Santi went back to his room and tried to phone Roz. She wasn't at home. Roz worked at the hospital. Sometimes she worked at night and sometimes in the day. Santi left a lot of messages. But she didn't call him.

***

Later, Santi was in the hotel bar. Gavin Harris came in. Gavin and Santi were old friends from Gavin's time at Newcastle. He played for Real now.

'You're going to hate Madrid,' laughed Gavin. 'No rain! No dark, cold mornings! Everyone speaks Spanish!'

'I know,' said Santi. 'But do I say "yes" or "no"?'

'What?! No one says "no" to Real Madrid.'

Santi looked at his friend and smiled. Gavin was right.

***

Santi arrived back at Newcastle Airport the next day.

'Hey, Santi! Is it true? Are you leaving Newcastle? Are you playing for Real Madrid now?'

People from the newspapers and TV were all around him. They wanted a good story.

When Santi got home, Roz was angry.

'Why didn't you talk to me first?' she said. 'You're going to Madrid! I heard it on the radio!'

'I tried to phone ...,' said Santi.

Roz went to work. She didn't say goodbye.

Santi felt terrible. 'I must speak to Roz,' he thought.

Santi went to the hospital. Roz was with Mr Ives. He wasn't well.

'So, you're going to Madrid,' said Mr Ives to Santiago. 'But don't take Roz! She's my favourite girl!'

'I'm not going, Mr Ives,' said Roz. 'Santiago didn't ask me. So I'm staying here.'

'Look, Roz,' said Santi. 'I love you, I want to be with you. But this is Real Madrid! It's so exciting.'

'But what about our house? And my job here at the hospital ... and ... I can't speak Spanish!' said Roz.

'You can stay here. You can visit me and I'll visit you. And I can teach you Spanish!' said Santiago.

'OK then,' smiled Roz. 'But I'm not eating paella!'

CHAPTER 3
Madrid

Santi arrived at the Real training ground – Gavin was already there. And so were Zidane, Raúl, Ronaldo and David Beckham – the best footballers in the world!

Some children watched and called to the players. The players smiled and called back.

***

Santi's first game for Real Madrid was against Olympiacos of Greece in the Champions League*. The Bernabéu+ was full.

Santiago sat next to Ronaldo. He was very nervous.

Who was in the team? And who was on the bench?

Far away in Los Angeles, Santi's grandmother Mercedes and his brother Julio waited for the match on TV. They sent Santi a text. He read it and thought of his father

* The top teams from each European country play in the Champions League. Thirty-two teams start. One wins.
\+ The Bernabéu is the home of Real Madrid. They play their games here.

Herman. Herman didn't like football. He was angry when Santi went to Newcastle. And Santi never talked to his father again, because Herman died. Before he died, he watched his son's first game on TV in a Los Angeles bar. And when Santi scored for Newcastle, he shouted to everyone in the bar, 'That's my son! Look! That's my son!'

But this was now. Roz was here at the Bernabéu and for Santi that was good.

***

Van der Merwe read out the names. Santi wasn't in the first eleven.

'Santiago Muñez, you are on the bench,' said Van der Merwe. 'But be ready to play.'

The game started. Santi watched every move.

Real played well. Zidane was great in the centre. And Beckham passed the ball well from the right. But after forty-five minutes, there were no goals. After eighty minutes, there were still no goals. Then Gavin was in front of the goal. He kicked the ball well … but it was high and it went over the top of the goal.

Then Santi heard his name. 'Muñez! You're on!' said the coach.

Santi ran on to the pitch. Gavin came off.

'This is it!' he thought. 'I'm playing for Real Madrid!'

The Real Madrid fans shouted Santi's name. The ball came to Santi. He was in the penalty box. 'I can't pass it,' he thought. 'There isn't time.' So he just kicked it. He kicked it first time, into the back of the goal. Everyone in the Bernabéu shouted.

Santi looked up at the sky. 'For you, Dad,' he said.

***

A woman worked in a little bar in Madrid. Her name was Rosa Maria. She watched Santi's goal on TV. Her son Enrique played football in the road.

'Listen,' she said to Enrique when he came in. 'See that footballer, Muñez? He started life with nothing … look at him now!'

'He had nothing? How do you know?'

'I know because ….' She moved near to her son and said something quietly in his ear. He looked at her.

'Is it true?' he asked.

'Yes,' she said. 'But don't tell anyone. You hear?'

CHAPTER 4

On the bench

Santiago loved scoring goals. He scored in training. He scored in games.

Burruchaga watched Santiago.

'He's very good. Why can't he start a game?' he asked the coach.

'Yes, he's good,' said Van der Merwe. 'But he isn't ready to start a game. He doesn't always pass the ball. He must learn first.'

The next Real game went badly. Gavin Harris usually scored a lot of goals. This time he didn't score any.

***

In the next La Liga* game, Gavin didn't score again.

'OK, Santi. Ready? You're going on,' said Van der Merwe.

'I can play 90 minutes!' Santi said as he ran past the coach. But Van der Merwe didn't answer.

The fans shouted. They were happy to see Santiago Muñez! It was nearly the end of the game when Santiago scored again! The Real fans shouted his name.

Burruchaga was right. Santi was a great goal scorer. But Van der Merwe knew his job. Santi was young. He was new. He must wait.

***

The Real Madrid players got a lot of money. They had big houses and fast cars. Gavin had a beautiful house with a lovely garden. And he gave a lot of parties.

* Football teams in Spain play in La Liga. Two of the top teams are Real Madrid and FC Barcelona.

'I'm having a party tonight,' Gavin said to Santi. 'And you are coming.'

Santi and Roz went to Gavin's party. Beautiful women talked and laughed with the players. Everyone wanted to talk to Santi. Santi was famous in Madrid.

Gavin gave Santi a drink. He had a tall, beautiful woman with him.

'This is Jordana,' Gavin said. 'She works in television.'

'Nice jacket,' said Jordana in Spanish. 'Is it Dolce*?'

'Yes,' said Santiago.

Just then Roz came back from the bathroom.

'You must come on TV with me,' Jordana said to Santi.

'Thanks, but no,' said Santiago.

'Did you just say "no" to me?' laughed Jordana.

'Roz, meet Jordana,' said Santi, in English.

But Roz felt angry. She didn't understand Spanish. 'What did she say to Santi?' she thought.

***

* Dolce & Gabbana is a famous Italian fashion house. Their clothes are very expensive.

Later, Roz asked Santi, 'Did you like that TV woman?'

Santi looked at Roz. 'Who? Jordana? No!' he said.

'But … she's beautiful and ….'

'I love you, remember?' he said.

But Roz was frightened. There were beautiful women everywhere. Santiago had a great job and now he had a lot of money. And women like rich footballers.

***

The next time Roz was in Madrid, Santi had a surprise for her. He took her to a beautiful big house.

'What do you think?' Santi asked Roz.

'You … you bought it?'

Santiago smiled. 'There are seven bedrooms. They all have bathrooms,' he said.

Roz followed Santi through white room after white room.

'Oh, look at the time. I must go,' he said. 'It's training time. Have fun!'

***

Roz sat in a bedroom and put on the TV. Two women talked about the Real game. One of the women was Jordana. Roz quickly turned the TV off.

Roz walked around the house. It was too big. She wanted to go home to Newcastle. It was OK here for Santi. He had his football, his friends. And he loved the money. Roz had nothing here. Just Santi. And now Santi wasn't here.

CHAPTER 5
'Goal!'

It was the next Champions League game. It was an important game against Rosenberg, a team from Norway. It was at the Bernabéu. A lot of fans were there. But Real Madrid didn't play well.

Beckham scored but then Rosenberg scored too and it was 1-1. Then Gavin got the ball. He was in front of the goal. He kicked the ball but it didn't go in. The fans shouted angrily. Van der Merwe called to him, 'Harris! You're off!'

It was bad for Gavin but it was good for Santiago.

Santi ran on to the pitch. He got the ball. He ran with it.

'Come on, Santi!' he thought. 'You can do this. You love scoring goals. You can win this game.'

Then he heard Van der Merwe.

'Pass the ball, Muñez!' he shouted. He was angry.

Santi passed. But then the ball came back to him. The referee looked at his watch. The game was nearly over. Santi looked up and saw only the goal. He kicked the ball.

'Goooaaalll!' shouted the fans.

After the game Van der Merwe talked to the team. He was not happy with Gavin.

'When are you going to score for me again?' he asked.

'I don't know, coach,' said Gavin, 'I'm not playing well.'

After the team talk, Santi talked to the coach.

'Look, *I'm* scoring,' he said. 'I'm ready to play 90 minutes.' Van der Merwe looked at him. He didn't smile.

'I choose the team, Muñez,' he said.

***

Roz was back in Newcastle. Santi called.

'I bought something. What do you think it is?'

'Go on.'

'A white Lamborghini*. It's so cool!'

Roz didn't say anything.

'Roz?' said Santi. 'Did you hear me?'

'Mr Ives died this morning,' she said.

'I'm sorry, Roz.'

'Me too,' said Roz.

***

Roz talked to her mother later.

'What's happening with you and Santi?' asked her mother. 'Santi's in Spain. You're here. It isn't good for you.'

'I know,' said Roz. 'Things are different now.'

'Roz,' said her mother. 'You must be there for him. You must be together. Go to Madrid. Talk to him.'

* A Lamborghini is a very expensive sports car.

CHAPTER 6
The photo

Santiago drove his Lamborghini across Madrid.

BANG! Something hit the car. Santi stopped.

A boy came to the window.

'I'm Enrique,' said the boy. 'I'm your brother.'

'What?' Santi didn't know this boy. 'What are you talking about?'

'We have the same mother. Your dad was Herman Muñez, in Mexico City, right?' said Enrique. 'You don't believe me? Look at this!' He gave Santi a photo. It was a woman, about forty years old, dark hair, dark eyes …

Santiago drove away. He was frightened.

'I must speak to Roz,' he thought. He called her on his mobile but she didn't answer.

He looked again at the photo. Black hair, brown eyes. 'Is this my mother?' he thought.

***

Santi got home at last. 'Why are the lights on?' he thought. He opened the door.

'I hope you're hungry.'

'Roz!' Santi smiled for the first time that day. He put his arms around Roz.

'I am very happy to see you,' he said.

They sat down. Roz gave him a drink.

'What's the matter?' asked Roz. 'Something's wrong.'

'Well,' Santi said. 'Today, a boy gave me this ...,' and he told her the story.

'Wow!' said Roz 'Do you think it's true?'

'I don't know. Maybe my mother *is* here in Madrid. Maybe it *is* true.'

'Or maybe this boy just wants money.'

'I can email the photo to my grandmother Mercedes,' said Santi suddenly. 'She knew my mother. She can tell me.'

***

Later, the phone rang. It was Mercedes.

'I got the photo,' she said. 'Yes, it's her. It's your mother.'

'She's in Madrid?' said Santiago. 'She's here in this city? Did you know? Why didn't you tell me?'

'Don't you remember?' Mercedes was angry. 'She left us, Santi. She left you. She left your father Herman. My poor son! He never smiled again!'

'But, Grandma —'

'Santi, stop. You mustn't see her.'

Santi put down the phone.

'I must see my mother,' he thought. 'I have questions. Why did she leave us? I want to know?'

CHAPTER 7
Everything goes wrong

Real had an important game against Valencia.

'Santiago,' said Van der Merwe, 'you're going to play 90 minutes today!'

When Santiago didn't smile, everyone was surprised.

'Why isn't he smiling?' asked Beckham.

'Maybe he's thinking about Gavin. He's got Gavin's place in the team,' said Zidane.

But Zidane was wrong.

***

Santiago ran onto the pitch. He tried to think about the game. But when Santi got the ball, a Valencia player took it from him. Santi was angry. He ran after the Valencia player.

'That's my ball!' he thought. He didn't look at the other players. He didn't think about his team.

He got to the Valencia player. He tried to kick the ball but he kicked the player. The player went down. Santi heard the referee's whistle. He looked around. The referee had a card in his hand … a red card!

***

The Real players often went to the Buddha bar. The music and dancing were great there.

Santi sat at the bar. He was alone. He watched the second part of the Valencia game on one of the big TVs. Gavin scored a goal. Santi smiled. It was his first smile today. But he didn't feel better.

'Hi, Santi!' It was Jordana. 'When are you coming on TV with me?' she asked. She smiled and sat next to him. They talked for a long time. Santi liked her. He didn't

think about the red card, the boy, the photo. He felt better.

'I must go,' said Santi. It was late.

'Yes, me too,' said Jordana. They walked out of the bar together.

'Bye,' said Santi. He kissed Jordana quickly.

Suddenly there were lights everywhere. Photographers!

'Great!' said Santi. He thought of the newspaper stories - Santi and Jordana, late at night, outside the Buddha bar.

***

Two days later Roz arrived in Madrid. She had a few days' holiday and she wanted to be there for Santi. Santi was in bed when she got to the house.

'Santi,' she said quietly. But he didn't wake up.

'He's very tired,' she thought. 'He thinks about his mother all the time. He must sleep.'

Later she made breakfast.

'Santi, Santi!' she said. 'Wake up! It's late.'

Suddenly Santi sat up. He looked at the clock.

'Roz!' he shouted angrily. 'Look at the time! Why didn't you wake me up?'

'I tried,' said Roz. 'But you were very tired.'

'I'm late for the team bus!' he shouted. 'We're flying to Norway. It's Rosenberg against Real. It's the Champions League!'

Santi dressed quickly and ran out of the house. He

didn't speak to Roz. He didn't say goodbye.

She heard the Lamborghini. Now Roz was angry.

'I'm not staying here,' she thought. 'I'm going home!'

***

It was very cold in Norway.

Van der Merwe was angry with Santiago. First there was the red card against Valencia. Then he didn't listen in training. And now he was late for the team bus.

The game against Rosenberg was difficult. The Real players did not usually play in cold weather. Gavin didn't play well and soon he came off. Santi stood up. He was ready to go on. But Van der Merwe didn't look at him. He didn't choose Santiago!

Santi was not happy. He was cold. Roz was angry with him. Van der Merwe was angry with him.

'And I'm on the bench!' he thought. 'Everything is going wrong.'

***

When Santi got home, the house was empty. Roz wasn't there. Santi was alone.

CHAPTER 8
Enrique's problem

Santiago told Gavin about his mother.

'What can I do?' he asked him. 'Why did she leave us? I must know.'

'You must find her,' said Gavin. 'And find her quickly. You're not playing good football. You're thinking about her too much.'

Gavin was right. But first Santi must find the boy.

***

Every day Santiago went to training. And every day he looked for the boy. And then he saw him! Santi was in his Lamborghini. He stopped next to the boy.

'Get in. I'm taking you home,' said Santi. The boy got in and Santi drove away.

'Now I can find my mother,' he thought.

Enrique looked around Santi's expensive car. There was his mobile, his watch, his sports bag.

'Hey, this mobile is cool!' he said.

He called a number. 'I'm phoning your coach,' he said. 'Hi, Van der Merwe. Can I play for Real? My brother plays for you!'

'Hey, stop that!' said Santi. 'What's your problem?'

'What's my problem?' said the boy angrily. 'Listen. My family is poor. My mum works all day and night. And you - my brother – you're driving around in a Lamborghini. You don't think about your family. *That's* my problem!'

Santi stopped at some lights. Suddenly Enrique was out of the car.

'I'm going,' he shouted. 'Thanks for this!' He had Santi's sports bag!

'Hey, wait,' called Santi. 'Where do you live?'

Too late. Santi hit the car window.

***

Santi drove to the Buddha bar. Gavin was there with other players from the team. Santi sat down next to them.

'Hey, Santi,' said Salgado. 'You phoned me three times. What's going on?'

'What?' asked Santi. 'But my mobile's in the car. Hey! Someone's in my car, with my phone!'

He ran back to the car park. Enrique was in his car. Too late again! Enrique drove away. Santiago called a taxi.

'See that car,' he said to the driver. 'That's my car! Follow it!'

The two cars drove fast through the streets of Madrid.

'Can he drive?' the taxi driver asked Santiago.

'I don't think so,' said Santi.

Santi was right. Enrique drove into a wall. The taxi stopped and Santi ran to Enrique. He looked bad. He put him in the taxi. 'Hospital! Quick!' he said to the driver.

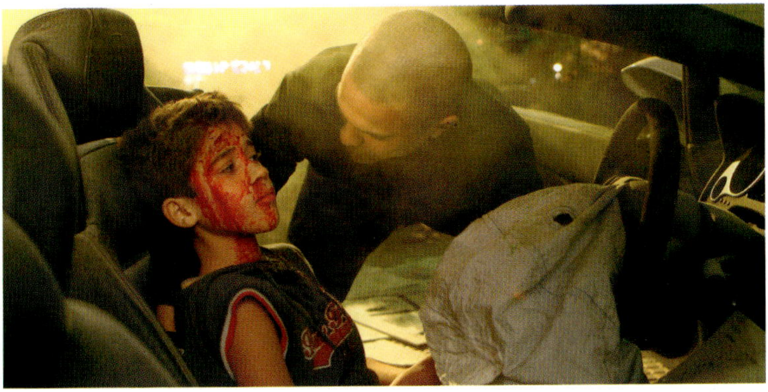

***

Photographers were at the hospital. They saw Santi and started to take pictures.

'Stop! Go away!' shouted Santi. One photographer put his camera in front of Santi's face. Santi hit him. The other photographers got great pictures. And five minutes later, Santi was in a police car.

Just then Rosa Maria arrived at the hospital. She saw Santiago. Santiago saw her. Then the police car drove away.

***

Santi stayed at the police station for the night.

He went home after some phone calls from the Bernabéu. When Santi got home, Roz called.

'There's a picture of you in a newspaper,' she said. 'It's you and Jordana. You're kissing her!'

The Buddha bar picture!

'But … nothing happened, Roz. We talked. I said good night. That's all,' said Santi. 'They want to sell a lot of newspapers. Their stories aren't true … .'

Roz put the phone down.

CHAPTER 9
The semi-final

The Champions League semi-final. Real went to Lyon for the first game. There were no goals and the game finished 0-0. Then Lyon came to Madrid.

'I think you're ready to play again, Santiago,' said Van der Merwe. 'But I'm putting you on the bench.'

'We must win this game,' Van der Merwe told the team. 'Real Madrid is not just a good team. It is a great team.'

Gavin was in the team. Gavin trained a lot these days. And he didn't go to parties every night.

'You're playing well again, Harris,' said Van der Merwe. 'Let's have some good goals today.'

The game started. Santiago watched. Gavin kicked the ball at the goal five times but it didn't go in. Then Real won a free kick. Beckham kicked the ball across the face of the goal. Gavin was in just the right place. It came down to his left foot and went into the goal. A fantastic goal!

'OK!' said Van der Merwe. 'Now you, Santi.'

Gavin came off, happy with his goal. Santi ran on. After all his mistakes, Santi wanted to play well. The ball came to him from Roberto Carlos. He turned quickly and left two Lyon players behind. He kicked the ball and it nearly went in. Santi got the ball again, this time from Ronaldo. He looked up, saw the goal and … it was 2-0!

The fans shouted and danced. They were so happy! They heard the referee's whistle for the end of the game. Yes! They were in the Champions League final!

***

This was Santi's dream. The biggest final in the world! He had everything. He played for Real Madrid. The fans loved him. He had houses in Madrid and Newcastle, a Lamborghini, beautiful clothes.

'Why does it all feel like nothing?' he thought.

***

Santi drove round the poor parts of Madrid. He showed the photo of his mother to everyone.

One man looked at the photo.

'Are you police?' he asked Santiago.

'No, I'm not. I just want to find her,' said Santi.

The man looked at Santi's watch.

'Nice watch,' he said. 'And I think I know this woman.'

***

It was evening. Santi got out of the taxi and looked at the bar. He felt nervous. But he must do this. He opened the door and went in. Everyone stopped drinking. They looked at the famous Real Madrid player.

Rosa Maria turned and looked at the door.

'Santiago!' she said quietly.

They didn't move for a moment. Then the footballer put his arms around his mother. She started to cry.

'Right, everyone, we're closing,' said Miguel, Rosa Maria's husband.

Santiago and his mother sat in the empty bar.

'Why did you leave us?' Santi asked his mother.

'One night, I came home late from work. It was dark. There were two men. They pulled me into a little street. One of the men was your uncle. He tried to kiss me. I ran to the house. Your father was there but I didn't say anything. The next night your uncle was there again. I ran away.'

'Why didn't you come for us?'

'Santiago,' said Rosa Maria. 'I came back three weeks later. You weren't there. A friend told me – your father took you to the US. And then, years later, I saw you on TV, here in Madrid. I wanted to phone you. But I was frightened. I'm so sorry.'

'Everything's going to be OK now,' said Santi. 'Hey! Where's Enrique? My new brother!'

***

Roz looked at her phone. It was a message from Santi.

'Roz! I met my mother. I know that money and fast cars are not important. You and my family are important. I'm sorry, Roz. Please call me, I love you.'

Roz wanted to tell Santi something too.

'We're going to have a baby,' she thought. 'And Santi doesn't know yet!'

CHAPTER 10
The final

Everyone talked about the Champions League final. 'Who will play?' they asked. 'Harris or Muñez?'

Santiago went into Van der Merwe's office. The coach looked up.

'Play Gavin in the final,' said Santi.

'What are you saying, Muñez?'

'I want to sit on the bench. Gavin is a good player. He wants to be in the England World Cup team. Maybe if he scores in this final ... .'

The coach didn't understand.

'I love football,' said Santi. 'But without my friends and family, it's nothing. When I came here I was excited. I wanted the money. I wanted to be famous. But all that isn't important. Gavin's my friend. Don't put him on the bench.'

***

Rosa Maria, Miguel and Enrique got into a taxi. Enrique had the Real shirts. Every shirt said 'Muñez' on the back. This was Santiago's new family. The taxi took them to the Bernabéu for the Champions League final!

In Los Angeles, Mercedes and Julio watched on TV.

At home in Newcastle, Roz and her mother watched too. Roz didn't want to fly now - the baby was too big.

Van der Merwe talked to the players. He read out the team.

'Zidane, Beckham, Guti, Robinho, Ronaldo,' he said. He read ten names and then he looked at Santi.

'Gavin Harris,' he said.

Gavin was surprised and happy, and Santi smiled too.

***

The players ran onto the pitch. They got to their places and they looked at the other team – one of the UK's top teams - Arsenal.

The referee started the game.

It was the worst start for Real. Arsenal scored in the first minute! The game was difficult. Arsenal played well. When the whistle went after 45 minutes, it was Real 0 Arsenal 1.

Van der Merwe talked to the players. He looked at Gavin.

'I'm coming off,' thought Gavin.

'OK, I want you up front,' said Van der Merwe. 'And

Santi is going to play behind you.'

When Santi ran on to the pitch, he thought, 'I'm playing for my family. All my family.'

***

But Thierry Henry soon had the ball for Arsenal. He ran fast with it, he went round four Real players and scored. Arsenal songs went round the Bernabéu.

There were only seven minutes left. Then Arsenal won a penalty kick.

In the Bernabéu, Rosa Maria took Enrique's hand. In Los Angeles, Mercedes took Julio's hand. In Newcastle, Roz took Carol's hand.

Casillas stood in the Real goal. The Arsenal player ran up to the ball. Everyone closed their eyes. He kicked the ball and Casillas stopped it! But there was no time …. Casillas quickly got the ball out to Santiago. Santiago kicked the ball up the pitch. Gavin ran after it. He was up in front of the Arsenal goal. Most of the Arsenal players were still at the Madrid end. Gavin kicked the ball and everyone watched. It went into the air and into the goal. Gavin didn't run to the fans. He took the ball back to the centre. Was there time to win?

The ball went from Zidane to Ronaldo to Beckham to Gavin. Real *must* score. The ball came to Santiago and he kicked it. It went into the goal! The Arsenal players didn't believe it.

Then Real won a free kick near the Arsenal penalty box. David Beckham put the ball down. The Bernabéu was quiet. Beckham ran up … he kicked the ball … everyone watched … mouths open … then the shouts started, 'Goooaaalll!!'

The referee looked at his watch. The whistle went. The game finished. Real 3 Arsenal 2. The sound in the Bernabéu was fantastic.

Gavin, Santiago and Beckham shouted and danced together.

Three players, three goals. Champions of Europe.

GOAL II: THE FILM

Q Are the films just about football?

A 'No,' says Kuno Becker. 'They are about friends. They are about love. And they are about dreams.' Kuno plays Santiago Muñez in all three *Goal* films.

Q Are there a lot of films about fooball already?

A Mike Jefferies and Jaume Collet-Serra made the *Goal* films. 'There are already films about most sports. But not about football,' says Mike. 'And it's the biggest sport in the world!'

Mike Jefferies wrote *Goal II*

Jaume Collet-Serra filming *Goal II*

A poor area of Mexico

Q Why doesn't a famous actor play Muñez?

A *Goal* is a story about a boy with nothing. He comes from a poor Mexican family. Mike and Jaume wanted people to believe the story. They didn't want a famous face. And they liked Kuno.

Q How did they film the football?

A They used real football games. They watched Newcastle and Real games. They saw good goals. Patrick Kluivert scored for Newcastle against Chelsea. They wanted this goal for the story. They filmed Kuno in Kluivert's place. When Santiago scores, the goal looks real. That's because it *is* real.

KUNO BECKER

Kuno comes from Mexico City. He was a musician before he was an actor. He played football at school but he didn't play very well. For the film, he trained four or five hours a day with a football coach.

Work in pairs. Do you like films about sport? Why/why not?

ANNA FRIEL

Anna comes from the north of England. She didn't like football before *Goal*. She saw her first football game at the Bernabéu. She's a fan now.

Anna likes Roz – Roz doesn't want to be on the front of all the magazines. She doesn't want to shop all day. She's a real person with a job and a life.

THE REAL FOOTBALLERS

Some of the real Real players are in *Goal II*. David Beckham and Zinedine Zidane speak to Santi in the film. We also see them in the dressing room and playing football. 'They were really friendly,' says Kuno. David Beckham has a bigger part in *Goal III*.

Did you know ...?
The film-makers asked Liverpool FC to do the *Goal* films. They said 'no'!

David Beckham

Zinedine Zidane

What do these words mean? You can use a dictionary.

actor dressing room film-maker magazine musician real

TOP TEAMS: NEWCASTLE

The fans: They are called the 'Toon army'. There are a lot of new Newcastle fans around the world because of the *Goal* films.

> “The Newcastle fans loved Santiago. He scored goals all the time.”

NEWCASTLE UNITED

Started: 1892.

The league: Newcastle play in the English Premiership in the UK.

The names: They are called 'the Magpies' because they wear black and white shirts. A magpie is a black and white bird.

The stadium: St James' Park. It's in the centre of the city. There are often 50,000 fans at the games here.

Famous players: Jackie Milburn, Alan Shearer and Michael Owen.

Michael Owen playing for 'the Magpies'

The city: Newcastle is in the north-east of England. It has famous old buildings and some very new buildings. The River Tyne runs through the middle.

Which famous footballer played for both teams?

AND REAL

REAL MADRID

Started: 1902.

The league: Real play in La Liga in Spain.

The names: They are called 'los merengues' (the meringues) because they wear white. They are also called 'los galácticos' because the club buys the most expensive players in the world.

The stadium: The Bernabéu. It's in the middle of Madrid. More than 80,000 fans can watch a game here.

Famous players: Where do we start!? Raúl, Ronaldo, Zinedine Zidane, David Beckham, Michael Owen, Fabio Cannavaro and Roberto Carlos are some of their famous footballers.

Ronaldo playing for 'los merengues'

The city: Madrid is Spain's largest city. The favourite sports here are football, basketball and bullfighting.

The fans: They are called 'madridistas'. Real has fans all over the world.

Discuss. Who's the most famous football team in your country? Are they your favourite team?

> "No one says 'no' to Real Madrid!"

What do these words mean? You can use a dictionary.

bullfighting competition league meringue stadium

CHAPTERS 1–3

Before you read

Use a dictionary for this section.

1 How much do you know about football? Put the words in the right places.

coach finals free kick penalty box
pitch Premiership

a) There are twenty teams in the English … .
b) There are twenty-two players on the … during a football game.
c) Jose Mourinho is a top football … .
d) The World Cup … happen every four years.
e) If Player A kicks Player B outside the …, Player B's team gets a … .

2 Match these words and meanings.

a) You feel this before you do something important or difficult.
b) You sit here if you are waiting to play in a game.
c) This person whistles at the end of the game.
d) These people travel all over the world with their team.

i) fans
ii) on the bench
iii) nervous
iv) referee

3 Read 'People and places' on pages 4–5. Answer these questions.

a) Santiago plays for Newcastle United. Is he going to play for a different club in *Goal II*, do you think?
b) Where do Santi's family live?
c) Which city do 'Geordies' come from?

After you read

4 Are these sentences right or wrong?

a) Glen Foy found Santiago in Newcastle and took him to Los Angeles.
b) Real Madrid wants to buy Santi from Newcastle.

c) Gavin thinks Santi is going to hate Madrid.
d) Roz is very happy about the job in Madrid.
e) Santi left Los Angeles and he didn't talk to his father again.
f) Santi played for the last ten minutes of the game against Olympiacos.

5 What do you think?
a) What does Rosa Maria say to her son in the bar?
b) How is life in Newcastle different from life in Madrid?

CHAPTERS 4–7

Before you read

6 Answer these questions.
a) Chapter 4 is called 'On the bench'. Who is going to be on the bench, do you think?
b) Chapter 5 is called 'Goal!' Who is going to score the goal?
c) Chapter 6 is called 'The photo'. Who is going to be in the photo?
d) Chapter 7 is called 'Everything goes wrong'. What is going to go wrong?

After you read

7 Who is it?
a) He usually scores a lot of goals. He likes parties.
b) She is beautiful. She works in television.
c) He buys a big house with seven bedrooms.
d) She thinks Roz must go to Madrid.
e) He has the same mother as Santi. He lives in a poor area of Madrid.
f) She doesn't want Santi to meet Rosa Maria.
g) He gets a red card against Valencia.
h) She kisses Santi outside the Buddha bar.
i) He doesn't play against Rosenberg.

8 What do you think?
Can life be difficult for people with a lot of money? How?

CHAPTERS 8–10

Before you read

9 Which of these things happen in the next part of the story, do you think?

a) Rosa Maria doesn't want to meet Santi.
b) Roz finds Rosa Maria and Enrique.
c) Mercedes flies to Madrid and stops Santi.
d) Roz see the photo of Santi and Jordana outside the Buddha bar.
e) Santi finds his mother.

10 Santi's mother left the family when Santi was a boy. Why did she leave, do you think? Talk to other students.

After you read

11 Put these events in order.

a) Enrique takes Santi's sports bag.
b) Gavin and Santi score in the semi-final against Lyon.
c) Enrique drives the Lamborghini into a wall.
d) Real Madrid win the Champions League.
e) Real score three goals in the last few minutes.
f) Santi and Gavin both play in the final.
g) Santi gives a man his watch and finds his mother.
h) Santi hits a photographer.
i) Santi takes him to hospital.
j) The police take Santi to the police station for the night.

12 What do you think?

a) How is Santi going to feel when he learns about the baby?
b) Is anything going to happen between Santi and Jordana?
c) Are Mercedes and Rosa Maria going to be friends?
d) Are you going to see *Goal III* to find the answers?